DOOMED HISTORY

CITY ON FIRE!

The Great Chicago Fire, 1871

by Nancy Dickmann

BEARPORT
PUBLISHING

Minneapolis, Minnesota

Credits: Front Cover, ©Library of Congress; 3, ©Library of Congress; 5, ©Everett Historical/ Shutterstock; 6, ©Photos BrianScant/Shutterstock; 7t, ©JamesAndrews1/Shutterstock; 7r, ©Brian Crawford from Oak Park, IL, USA/Public Domain; 8, ©The Western News Company, Chicago/Public Domain; 9, ©FLHC44/Alamy; 10, ©A.H. Abbott/Public Domain; 11, ©Science History Images/Alamy; 12–13, ©Chicago Illustrated/Newberry Library; 14, ©Library Of Congress; 15, ©javi4x4/Shutterstock; 16, ©Julia Pachyzhna/Shutterstock; 17, ©Nagel Photography/Shutterstock; 18, ©Todd Bannor/Alamy; 19, ©Currier and Ives/ Chicago Historical Society/Public Domain; 20, ©Library of Congress; 21,©New York Public Library/Public Domain; 22, ©Library of Congress; 23, © Library of Congress; 24, ©C.R. Clark Photograph/Newberry Library/Public Domain; 25, ©History Museum of Chicago/City of Chicago/Public Domain; 26, ©ChicagoPhotographer/Shutterstock; 27, ©Everett Historical/Shutterstock; 28–29, ©AindriuH/Shutterstock.

Bearport Publishing Company Product Development Team
President: Jen Jenson; Director of Product Development: Spencer Brinker; Senior Editor: Allison Juda; Editor: Charly Haley; Associate Editor: Naomi Reich; Senior Designer: Colin O'Dea; Associate Designer: Elena Klinkner; Associate Designer: Kayla Eggert; Product Development Assistant: Anita Stasson

Brown Bear Books
Children's Publisher: Anne O'Daly; Design Manager: Keith Davis; Picture Manager: Sophie Mortimer

Library of Congress Cataloging-in-Publication Data

Names: Dickmann, Nancy, author.
Title: City on fire! : the Great Chicago Fire, 1871 / by Nancy Dickmann.
Other titles: Great Chicago Fire, 1871
Description: Minneapolis, Minnesota : Bearport Publishing Company, [2023] | Series: Doomed history | Includes bibliographical references and index.
Identifiers: LCCN 2022046065 (print) | LCCN 2022046066 (ebook) | ISBN 9798885093941 (library binding) | ISBN 9798885095167 (paperback) | ISBN 9798885096317 (ebook)
Subjects: LCSH: Great Fire, Chicago, Ill., 1871--Juvenile literature. | Fires--Illinois--Chicago--History--19th century--Juvenile literature. | Chicago (Ill.)--History--To 1875--Juvenile literature.
Classification: LCC F548.42 .D53 2023 (print) | LCC F548.42 (ebook) | DDC 977.3/11041--dc23/eng/20220927
LC record available at https://lccn.loc.gov/2022046065
LC ebook record available at https://lccn.loc.gov/2022046066

© 2023 Brown Bear Books

This edition is published by arrangement with Brown Bear Books.

North American adaptations © 2023 Bearport Publishing Company. All rights reserved. No part of this publication may be reproduced in whole or in part, stored in any retrieval system, or transmitted in any form or by any means, electronic, mechanical, photocopying, recording, or otherwise, without written permission from the publisher.

For more information, write to Bearport Publishing, 5357 Penn Avenue South, Minneapolis, MN 55419.

CONTENTS

CITY ON THE RISE

A sprawling new city was bustling to life in the heart of the United States. It seemed like nothing could stop Chicago's rise.

When the United States was first becoming independent, Chicago was just a small trading post in the wilderness. But by 1850, more than 30,000 people lived there. **Canals** and railroads linked the growing city to both coasts, with Chicago acting as a stop along the way. Grain and livestock from farms in the west passed through the city on their way to the east. Many **immigrants** came looking for work, swelling Chicago's population even more.

In the City

Chicago was full of **warehouses**, cattle yards, grain **silos**, railroad lines, and factories. It was becoming a city of wealth and entertainment, too. Wealthy visitors stayed in lavish hotels. People could shop at fancy department stores and go to concert halls lit by **gaslight**.

By 1871, about 300,000 people lived in Chicago. It was the fifth-largest city in the United States.

5

THE FIRST SIGNS OF TROUBLE

After a scorching summer, fall wasn't letting up as hot weather and dry conditions left Chicago primed for disaster. It wasn't long before the city would be in flames.

Throughout the entire summer of 1871 only an inch (2.5 cm) of rain fell on Chicago. Fall hadn't started much better. In addition to being unusually warm for the season, October brought very strong winds whipping through the streets. These were perfect conditions for a fire—only a spark was needed to set it off.

Chicago stands on the shores of Lake Michigan, but despite the water, summers can be hot and dry.

Many of Chicago's first roads were paved with wooden blocks.

City of Wood

It wasn't just the weather that made Chicago the perfect setting for a fire. Most of the city's buildings were made of wood. When Chicago's population boomed, all those people needed homes. Houses made of wood were the quickest and cheapest to build. Even the buildings made of stone or brick often had wooden walls, ceilings, and staircases inside. What's more, Chicago had about 600 miles (1,000 km) of wooden sidewalks.

One after Another

With so much dry wood around, fires were common in Chicago's early days. More than 500 fires were reported in Chicago in 1868. In October 1871, the dry weather caused fires to break out every day. There were four fires on October 5 and another five the next day. On the night of October 7, the city's already-exhausted firefighters spent hours fighting a blaze that burned four city blocks. The fire department needed more people and better equipment. They weren't prepared for what would happen next.

Chicago's fire department had about 185 firefighters in 1871. They used horse-drawn vehicles.

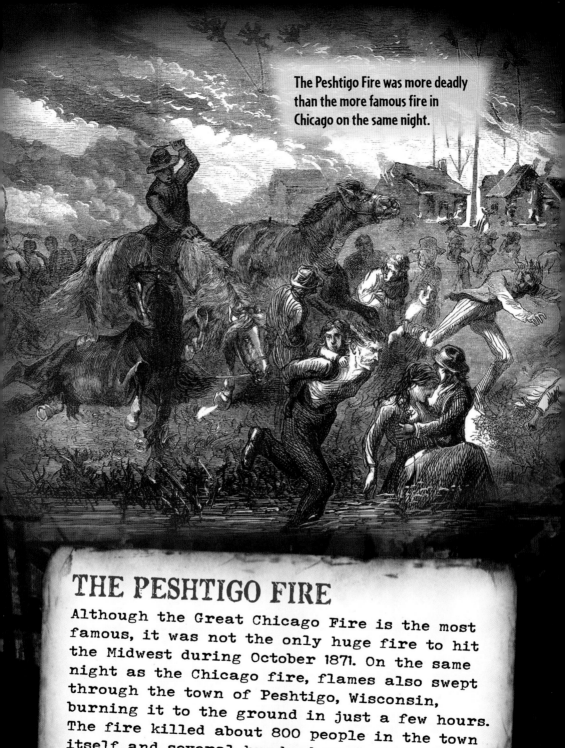

The Peshtigo Fire was more deadly than the more famous fire in Chicago on the same night.

THE PESHTIGO FIRE

Although the Great Chicago Fire is the most famous, it was not the only huge fire to hit the Midwest during October 1871. On the same night as the Chicago fire, flames also swept through the town of Peshtigo, Wisconsin, burning it to the ground in just a few hours. The fire killed about 800 people in the town itself and several hundred more in the surrounding area.

Mrs. O'Leary's Barn

Catherine and Patrick O'Leary lived with their children in a small wooden house on DeKoven Street, in the southwest part of Chicago. On Sunday, October 8, at about 8:30 p.m., a fire started in a barn behind their house.

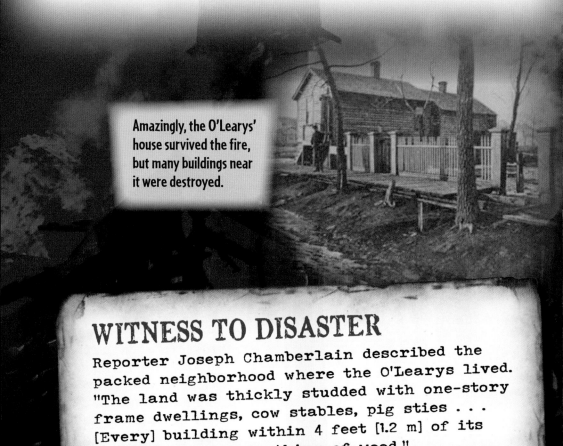

Amazingly, the O'Learys' house survived the fire, but many buildings near it were destroyed.

WITNESS TO DISASTER

Reporter Joseph Chamberlain described the packed neighborhood where the O'Learys lived. "The land was thickly studded with one-story frame dwellings, cow stables, pig sties . . . [Every] building within 4 feet [1.2 m] of its neighbor, and everything of wood."

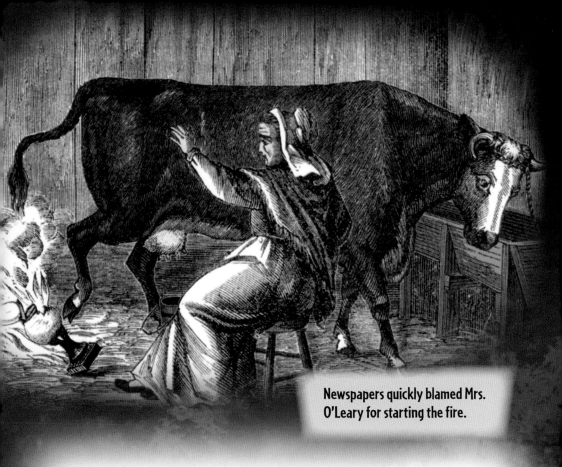

Newspapers quickly blamed Mrs. O'Leary for starting the fire.

Was It a Cow?

After the disaster, people spread stories that the fire started when a cow that Mrs. O'Leary was milking kicked over a lantern. Was that a fair accusation? Probably not. Mrs. O'Leary said she was in bed when the barn burst into flames. The fire may have been started by a spark blown from a nearby chimney, or there may have been a thief in the barn who knocked over a lantern while trying to steal milk. No one will ever know for sure.

DISASTER STRIKES

The fire started small, but soon flickering flames could be seen across the city. The burning disaster spread quickly.

On that night of October 8, a watchman in the tall tower on top of Chicago's courthouse spotted the fire and told the fire department. But he gave the wrong location! By the time he realized his mistake, the firefighters had already been sent to a neighborhood about 1 mile (1.6 km) away from the O'Learys' barn.

Too Late

While the firefighers were searching for the true source of the flames, the fire spread. By the time they reached the area of the fire just before 10:00 p.m., it had been more than an hour after the O'Learys' barn burst into flames. The fire was now out of control, burning everything in its path.

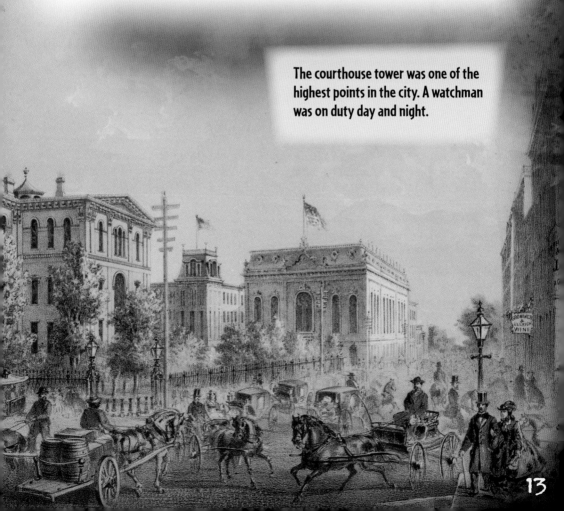

The courthouse tower was one of the highest points in the city. A watchman was on duty day and night.

The flames spread to several sawmills full of wood, which made the fire grow even larger.

Wind and Fire

A strong wind blowing from the southwest pushed the fire along. The firefighters could not keep up with nature. Thanks to the lack of rain, the wooden buildings and sidewalks burst into flames easily. The wind carried burning sparks and **embers**, setting new buildings on fire every minute. People in the area began to flee for their lives.

A Slim Hope

There were two natural **firebreaks** in the path of the blaze. The Chicago River to the east and an area previously destroyed by a small fire along the north should have slowed the spread. In normal conditions, these areas where there was nothing to feed the flames may have even stopped the fire. But the strong wind blew burning material straight across these firebreaks. By 11:30 p.m., the fire had jumped the river and moved past the area burned the day before. It kept heading north.

A firebreak is an area where there is nothing that can catch fire, so flames have nothing to burn and can't spread.

LIFE OR DEATH

The fire kept moving, destroying everything in its path. Soon, it hit the city's **gasworks** building, adding literal fuel to the fire.

Around midnight, the city's gasworks caught fire and a tank of gas exploded. With the gas supply gone, the city lost the ability to power its lights, leaving everything in darkness. The blazing flames provided the only light as people ran for their lives.

Like many cities, Chicago had a network of pipes to deliver gas to streetlights, businesses, and homes.

The Field & Leiter store in Chicago was a popular shopping destination, full of flammable goods.

Moving Merchandise

At the fancy Field & Leiter department store, employees used delivery wagons to move their **merchandise** to safety. When the lights went out, they worked by candlelight and escaped just before the building burst into flames. Nearby, the courthouse also caught fire. The people held in its prison cells were released to run for their lives. It didn't take long for both the store and the courthouse to burn to the ground.

Downtown in Flames

The fire had burned through the edge of the city and everything built along the Chicago River. As it moved into the city center, offices and stores started to burst into flames as well.

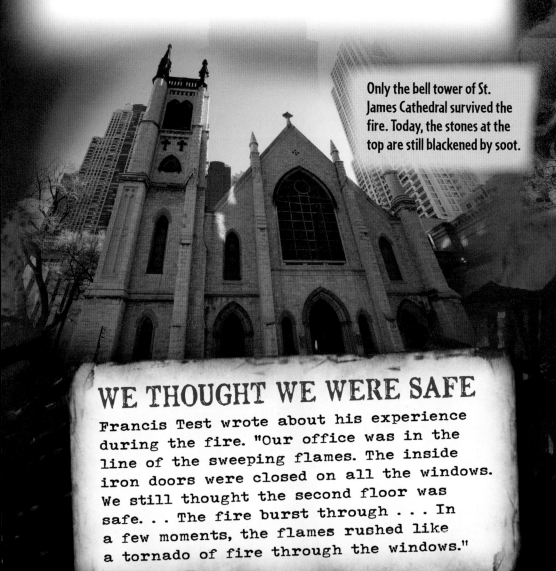

Only the bell tower of St. James Cathedral survived the fire. Today, the stones at the top are still blackened by soot.

WE THOUGHT WE WERE SAFE

Francis Test wrote about his experience during the fire. "Our office was in the line of the sweeping flames. The inside iron doors were closed on all the windows. We still thought the second floor was safe. . . The fire burst through . . . In a few moments, the flames rushed like a tornado of fire through the windows."

The city's bridges were crowded with panicking people.

Over the Bridge

People packed into horse-drawn wagons and rushed away on foot to escape the spreading fire. They crowded onto bridges—the only ways to cross the river that cuts through the middle of the city. Meanwhile, efforts to stop the fire were getting more desperate. At about 3:00 a.m., the city's **waterworks** system was destroyed. Waterwork pumps that sent water across the city had been the last chance of stopping the flames.

Moving North

All those people were trying to flee the same direction—north. They had nowhere else to run. The fire was raging in the city's southern and central areas. To the east, Lake Michigan blocked any escape. As flames licked closer to the lakeshore, many who ran in that direction were trapped.

People ran for their lives as smoke poured from the windows of the burning buildings.

SCENES OF DISASTER

A woman who was visiting Chicago when it burst into flames wrote, "Our boys ran at full speed, and we followed, crossing State Street Bridge amid a shower of coals. . . The crowd thickened every moment."

Firebreak

With water gone and more of the city to save, Philip Sheridan, an army general stationed in Chicago, ordered his troops to blow up buildings in the fire's path. By removing the buildings, he thought there would be nothing left for the fire to burn. Unfortunately, this did not stop the fire but instead destroyed even more of the city's homes.

Between flames and explosives, many of the city's residents were left without homes.

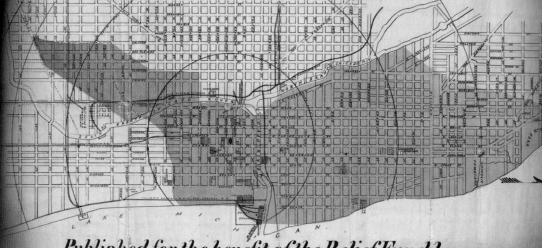

MAP SHOWING THE BURNT DISTRICT IN CHICAGO!

Published for the benefit of the Relief Fund by
3ᴰ EDITION. THE R.P.STUDLEY COMPANY, ST. LOUIS.

By October 9, a huge area of the city had been destroyed by fire.

Still Running

Many people in the northern part of the city had stayed in their homes, thinking that the fire couldn't cross the river. But by the afternoon of October 9, they had to flee and head for the open prairies north of the city. Some of them buried valuable items before they left their homes, hoping to dig them up after the danger had passed.

ESCAPE TO THE WEST

Lambert Tree escaped on a horse-drawn grocery wagon. "I soon bargained with its driver to take as many as we could get into it to the west side for $10. The smoke was still so dense that we could [not see much] but we saw enough to know that the north side at least was destroyed."

Burning Out

The fire had consumed so much of the city that it was running out of things to burn. Rain also started to fall, which helped put out the remaining flames. By next morning, the fire was over, but most of the city was destroyed.

Only ruins remained in many places by the time the fire was over.

WHAT HAPPENED NEXT

The fire was finally out, but only rubble remained where a proud city once grew. Chicago was changed forever.

Much of the city now lay in ruins. More than 17,000 buildings had been destroyed, along with many miles of wooden streets and sidewalks. About 300 people died in the fire, and many of the survivors lost everything they owned. More than 100,000 people— one-third of Chicago's population—were now homeless.

News photographers toured the city after the fire was out, taking pictures of the destruction.

Charity groups and the city government quickly found ways to help people who lost their homes.

TO THE HOMELESS.

The Head Quarters of the **General Relief Committee** are at the

CONGREGATIONAL CHURCH,

Cor. Washington & Ann Sts.,

All of the Public School Buildings, as well as Churches, are open for the shelter of persons who do not find other accommodations. When food is not found at such buildings it will be provided by the committee on application at Head Quarters.

R. B. MASON, Mayor.
J. H. McAVOY, South Division.
N. K. FAIRBANK, do.
W. B. BATEHAM, West Division. } General Relief Committee.
ORRIN E. MOORE, do.
M. A. DEVINE, North Division.
JOHN HERTUNG, do.
C. T. HOTCHKISS, Secretary.

Chicago, October 10, 1871.

Helping the Homeless

Chicago's mayor was worried about **looting** and violence, so he asked General Sheridan to put the city under **martial law** for two weeks. The army made sure food and water was shared, and they stopped people from stealing from burned or **abandoned** buildings. People from all over the country sent money and supplies to help the survivors.

A NEW LIBRARY

Before the fire, Chicago had libraries where people had to pay to borrow the books. The fire destroyed about two million books across the city. People in the United Kingdom donated about 8,000 new ones. This gift helped create Chicago's first free public library.

Rebuilding

There was never a question whether Chicago would be rebuilt. Work started immediately. Despite the disaster, the city pushed forward.

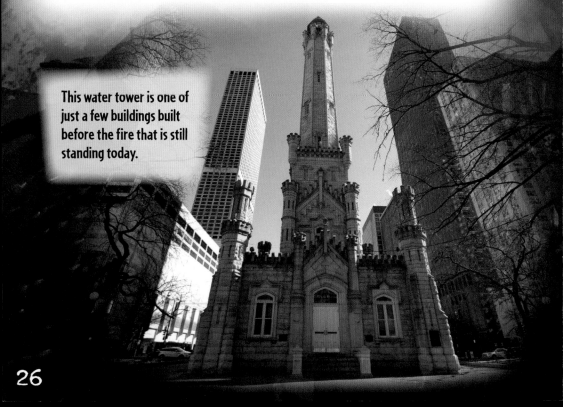

This water tower is one of just a few buildings built before the fire that is still standing today.

The World's Fair showed off new technology. This was where many visitors saw electric lights for the first time ever.

The New City

The fire taught the people of Chicago some valuable lessons, and they were determined to make their new city better than the old one. The city government drafted new fire regulations, including a rule that said buildings in the central business district had to be made of stone or brick. With all the rebuilding and growth, the city's population swelled to 500,000 people by 1880. In 1893, Chicago hosted a World's Fair to show to the world how it had risen from the ashes.

Building Better

City planners and **architects** worked to improve Chicago's waterworks and to build new railroads. Advances in technology, including elevators and steel building frames, meant structures could be made stronger and taller than ever before. Architects flocked to Chicago, eager to design office buildings in the city center and **modern** homes for residents who decided to move to the suburbs after the fire.

Chicago has taken its place as one of the world's great cities, but the fire will always be remembered.

A Sad Ending

What about Mrs. O'Leary? She and her family survived, but for the rest of her life she was blamed for the fire. Reporters **harassed** her, and people shouted at her in the streets. Mrs. O'Leary died in shame in 1895. More than 100 years later, the Chicago City Council finally officially announced Mrs. O'Leary wasn't to blame.

KEY DATES

1871

October 5–7 Chicago's firefighters battle several blazes throughout the city.

October 8

8:30 p.m. A fire starts in the O'Learys' barn.

10:00 p.m. The first firefighters arrive on the scene.

11:30 p.m. The fire jumps the Chicago River and continues north and east.

October 9

12:00 a.m. The fire reaches the city gasworks building.

1:00 a.m. The courthouse begins to burn.

3:00 a.m. The pumps at the city's waterworks are destroyed.

10:00 a.m. The army blows up buildings to try and stop the fire.

October 10 Rain begins to fall and helps put out the fire.

1893

May 1 The World's Fair opens in Chicago, showing off the newly rebuilt city.

1997

October 6 The Chicago City Council votes to announce Mrs. O'Leary was not to blame for the fire.

QUIZ How much have you learned about the Great Chicago Fire? It's time to test your knowledge! Then, check your answers on page 32.

1. **Where did the fire start?**
   a) in a house
   b) in a barn
   c) in a sawmill

2. **What mistake did the watchman on the courthouse tower make?**
   a) he fell asleep and didn't see the fire
   b) he forgot to ring the warning bell
   c) he sent the firefighters to the wrong location

3. **What were most of the city's sidewalks made of?**
   a) wood
   b) gravel
   c) asphalt

4. **What did the city's streetlights run on?**
   a) electricity
   b) gas
   c) solar power

5. **How did the army try to stop the fire?**
   a) by blowing up buildings to create a firebreak
   b) by collecting water from the lake
   c) by blocking the bridges

GLOSSARY

abandoned left behind

architects people who design buildings

canals human-made waterways that allow boats to travel between natural bodies of water

embers small pieces of burning wood

firebreaks areas where there is nothing to burn, providing stopping points for fires

gaslight an old system of lighting using gas to create a bright flame

gasworks a building where a city's gas supply is produced, stored, and sent out for delivery to homes and businesses

harassed bothered or bullied

immigrants people who move to live in another country

looting stealing things from ruined or abandoned buildings during or after a disaster

martial law a situation in which the army is put in charge of a place during an emergency

merchandise goods that are bought or sold

modern a style that is new and different from styles of the past

silos towers used to store grain

warehouses large buildings where goods are stored

waterworks a set of pumps and other mechanisms that control a city's water supply

INDEX

READ MORE

Hannigan, Kate. *The Great Chicago Fire: Rising from the Ashes* (*History Comics*). New York: First Second Books, 2020.

Lewis, Mark L. *Fire Rescues* (*Rescues in Focus*). Lake Elmo, MN: Focus Readers, 2020.

Perdew, Laura. *The 12 Worst Fires of All Time* (*All-Time Worst Disasters*). Mankato, MN: 12-Story Library, 2019.

LEARN MORE ONLINE

1. Go to **www.factsurfer.com** or scan the QR code below.

2. Enter **"City on Fire"** into the search box.

3. Click on the cover of this book to see a list of websites.

Answers to the quiz on page 30
1) B; 2) C; 3) A; 4) B; 5) A